Nola

Nola

Written by Stephanie Lisa Tara

Illustrated by Pilar Lama

Preserve. Conserve. Inspire. Teach.

Stephanie Lisa Tara
CHILDREN'S BOOKS

Nola is the story of the last American Northern White Rhino. Today, only three are left on the planet. Nola was rescued from her African savanna as a child by the good, kind folks at San Diego Zoo Safari Park. Poaching has decimated Nola's species due to the fallacy that rhino horns are thought to possess magical medicinal powers. They do not. Nevertheless . . . rhino horns are big business. Extinction is an ugly word. Greed is an uglier word. What to do? Understand what happened to Nola and her kind. Learn the lessons that Nola teaches us. And then, tell our children Nola's story using gentle, evocative language that invites compassion, inspiration and awareness.

Nola

Stephanie Lisa Tara Children's Books
San Francisco, California

Preserve. Conserve. Inspire. Teach.

ISBN Hardback: 978-0-9894334-8-8
ISBN Paperback: 978-0-9894334-9-5
ISBN E-book: 978-0-615-93437-2

Printed in the United States.
10 9 8 7 6 5 4 3 2 1

For more information about the author, or the book, please visit: www.stephanielisatara.com.

Preserve. Conserve. Inspire. Teach.

Stephanie Lisa Tara
CHILDREN'S BOOKS

For Nola

whose grace and courage inspires us all

And for Madeline

whose good heart makes her mother so very proud

Nola

Stephanie Lisa Tara founded a publishing company that empowers kids to care about the planet, themselves and each other. Her creed is activism, inspiring the next generation to make the world a better place. Adults love her books because they help explain 'stuff' in gentle, giggly ways. Kids love her books because they are super fun to read. Who is Stephanie? A San Francisco mom with a great big heart. As a child she had bright red hair, a little too bright in fact. Being different got Stephanie thinking...our differences are the celebration! Whether scaly, feathered, furry, or human-skinned; we all call Earth home. Lyrical prose that dances on our tongue, breathtaking watercolors that illume our imaginations...these are the hallmarks of Stephanie's work. PRESERVE. CONSERVE. INSPIRE. TEACH. We've only one planet to save.

Born in Madrid, Spain, **Pilar Lama** has always loved to draw and paint. With a specialized education in children's illustration, she uses several techniques: pencil, watercolor, acrylic, gouache and digital. Pilar is an outgoing kind, happy hard-worker and is a very imaginative person. She is married and has a three year old who serves as her inspiration. Pilar has a special skill for creating adorable and endearing characters and for transforming well-known characters into her unique style. Her drawings are characterized by their wide range of bright luminescent colors that show the passion she gives to each of her creations. When she's not working on commissioned illustrations, she is writing and developing illustrations for her own books. She never stops dreaming up new ideas. Pilar is represented by WendyLynn & Co.

Tom Hamlyn loves his cats George & Rabbit! And Tom loves Rhinos too! So he felt very lucky to be asked to create the animated lyrical lettering you'll see here in celebration of Nola and her story. Inspired by Stephanie's previous book *I'll Follow the Moon* and Pilar's delightful paintings Tom set about designing a fun, easy to ready typography, that would compliment the artwork while accenting Stephanie's wonderful text in just the right way.

Tom is an artist & designer originally from the UK. He grew up in the British countryside where his family set up a Pottery and he learned not to be afraid of the dark by walking at night listening to the sounds of animals and looking at the moon. Perhaps Nola did that too.

Why did the world love Nola? Was it her kind, loving eyes? Her unique sense of humor? The way she trotted up to her visitors at Safari Park, greeting each and every one. Perhaps it was her ancient age that had us in love with her, a matriarch with the endearing lined skin of a grandmother. Or maybe, it was her courage. Maybe this was why world leaders paused to mark her death on November 22, 2015. Why Nola's name made world headlines. Newspapers. Television. Internet. Nola, Nola, Nola. The very last of her kind. With only three relatives left alive in Kenya. Maybe it was Nola's courage to be the last that had us loving her, weeping at her loss. Courage to be the last with grace, humility, and forgiveness. Extinction is forever. Nola knew this. She forgave us, I think. She only asks that we honor her story.

It was a hot summer afternoon in August 2015, even for San Diego, yet my daughter and I barely felt the heat. We stood in our safari truck, gripping binoculars. Where was she? We had been traveling along the savanna for an hour now. Suddenly we heard heavy footsteps and a silhouette appeared on the horizon. Grey, rounded, enormous. There stood Nola! World famous northern white rhino, the very last of her kind here in America, one of four left on the planet, her species almost extinct. "Nola!" my eleven year old cried. At hearing her name, Nola sped toward our truck. Hearts thumping, cameras replaced binoculars. I leaned over the edge of the truck and looked into her eyes. How can I explain this moment? Deep-set, brown eyes that did not flinch from mine. At all. I held my gaze and so did she. 'Are you afraid', I whispered. 'No, I am not', she seemed to say back to me, her ears fluttering a little, her eyes deepening their stare. As our truck pulled away I said to my child, "I'm going to write Nola's story, Maddie."

And so I have.

With love,
Stephanie Lisa Tara

Love your Horn

It makes you, you—
Your horn is your heart
Nola, it's true!

*You will always be loved little rhino, it's true
Now and forever... I promise you!*

Some Have Stripes

Feathers, fur, spots,
But rhinos have horns,
Horns matter lots!

You will always be loved little rhino, it's true
Now and forever... I promise you!

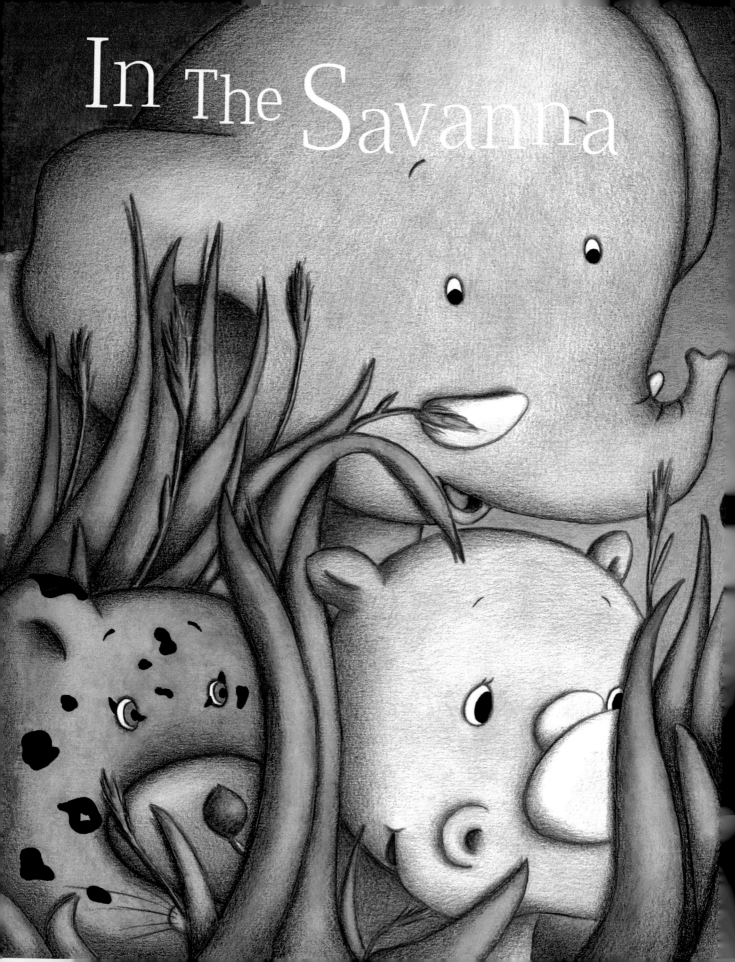

You will always be loved little rhino, it's true
Now and forever... I promise you!

Yellow-brown grass,
We play all day long
The hours pass.

GROW GROW

GROW

GRO

I learn so much,
Listen, remember
See, smell, and touch!

W

You will always be loved little rhino, it's true
Now and forever... I promise you!

I
Love
Mud!

Sticky! Let's play,
Get ready to jump...
SPLASH! Fun! Hooray!

You will always be loved little rhino, it's true
Now and forever... I promise you!

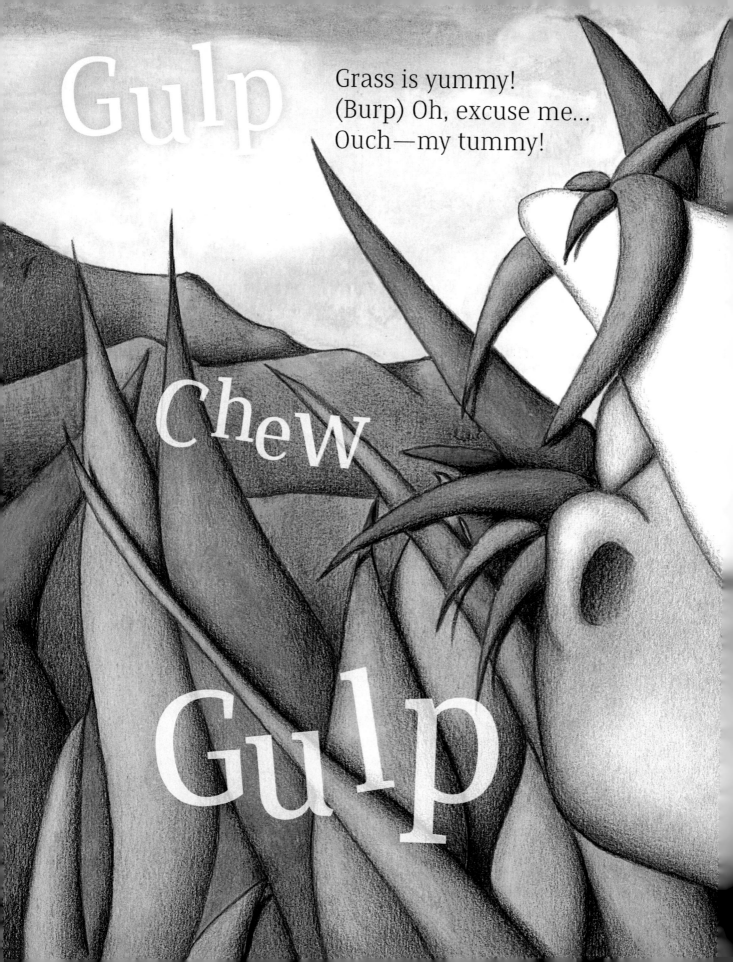

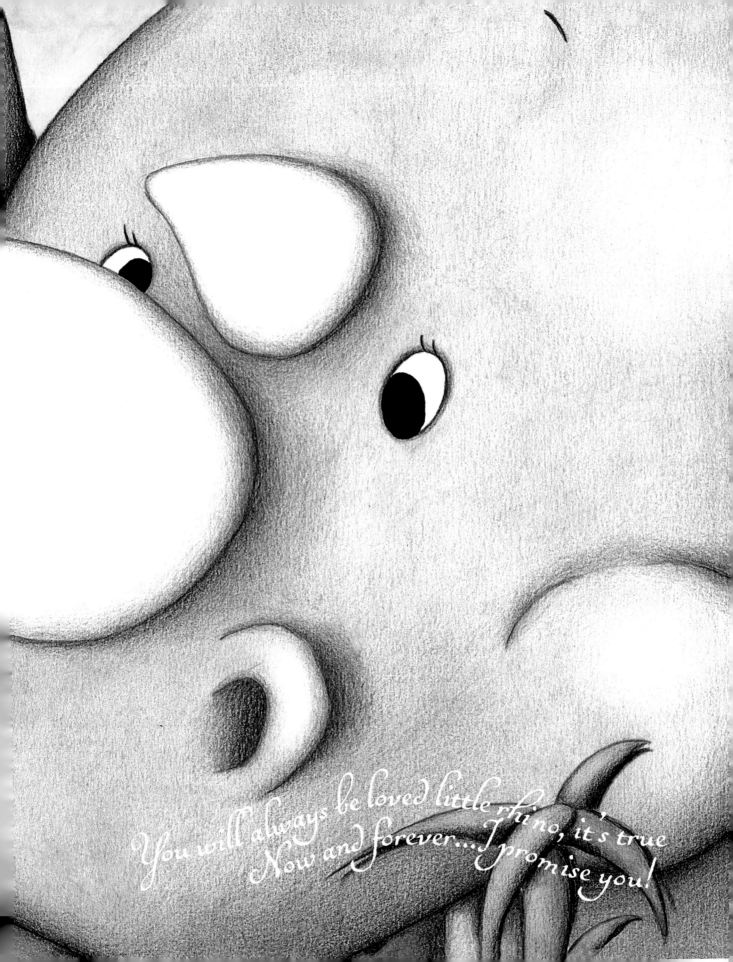

You will always be loved little rhino, it's true
Now and forever...I promise you!

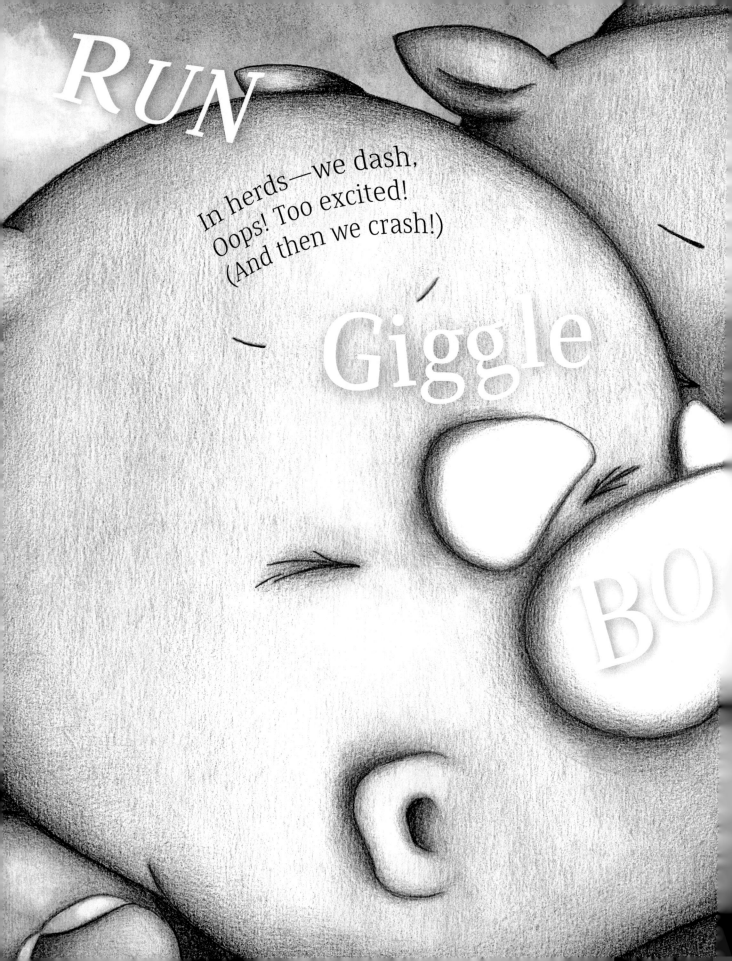

RUN

In herds—we dash,
Oops! Too excited!
(And then we crash!)

Giggle

BO

You will always be loved little rhino, it's true
Now and forever... I promise you!

Then One Day

A shadow fell,
Oh, what a surprise...
When all was well.

You will always be loved little rhino, it's true
Now and forever...I promise you!

They want your horn!
It sure sounds silly...
(Grassland friends warn)

*You will always be loved little rhino, it's true
Now and forever...I promise you!*

That's His Trunk

Those are her wings?
They wear their own stripes!
These are OUR things!

Who would Want

What wasn't theirs?
Too silly for words!
Too odd for cares!

*You will always be loved little rhino, it's true
Now and forever... promise you!*

Try To Hide

Behind a tree,
My body's too big!
Can you see me?

You will always be loved little rhino, it's true
Now and forever... I promise you!

Her face is kind,
Come here l'il rhino...
If you don't mind?

You will always be loved little rhino, it's true
Now and forever... I promise you!

Smile at Me

I smile at you,
Friendship is something
Between just two.

You will always be loved little rhino, it's true
Now and forever... I promise you!

Ha! Ha! Ha!

Yes, I'm ticklish!
Okay, I trust you...
I'll go! Your wish!

You will always be loved little rhino, it's true
Now and forever...I promise you!

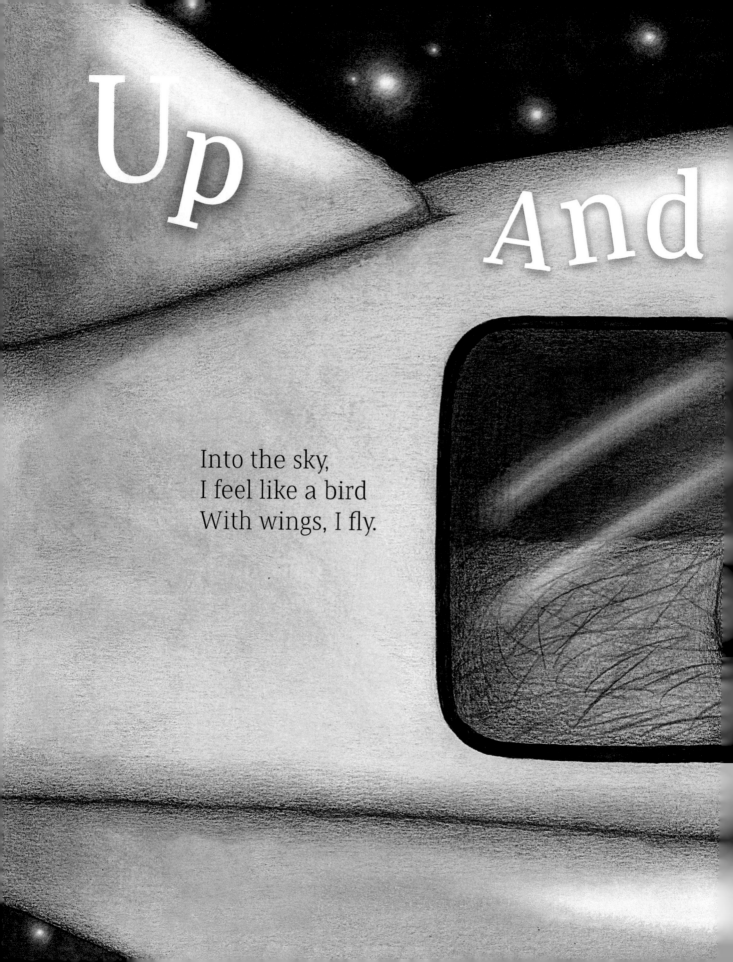

Up And

Into the sky,
I feel like a bird
With wings, I fly.

Away

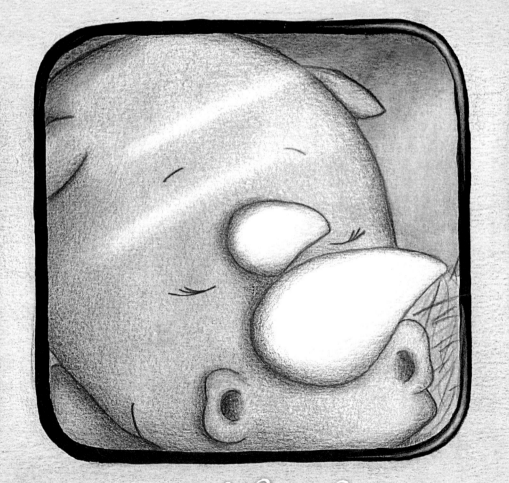

You will always be loved little rhino, it's true
Now and forever...I promise you!

You will always be loved little rhino, it's true
Now and forever...I promise you!

soOn I Learn

About my fame,
And why all the world
Now knows my name...

Please
Listen
Close

Bring your ear, near,
For what I must say
Must be quite clear...

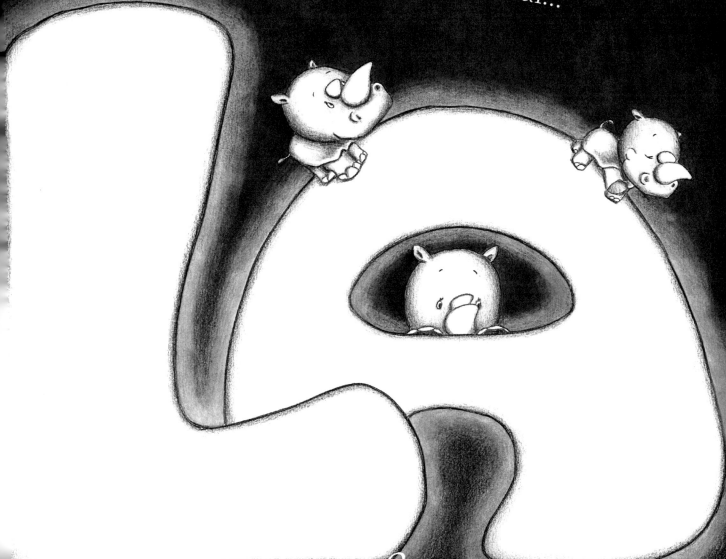

You will always be loved little rhino, it's true
Now and forever... I promise you!

I'm

The

Last

Here at this zoo,
Northern White Rhinos
Are down to few...

I
Have
Hope

That this will change,
The world loves rhinos!
It sure seems strange.

You will always be loved little rhino, it's true
Now and forever...I promise you!

You Ask Why?

The truth is this,
Some want, what's not theirs
(And there it is.)

So My Friends

Here's what I say,
Let us all join hands
It's a new day!

I'm happy

We'll love on

Promise Me Now

One giant thing:
Go out to the world!
YOUR TURN TO SING!

I'm me, you're happy, you're you, another... yes, that's what we'll Do!

Nola

My favorite scripture is "Ask the animals, they will teach you . . ." JOB 12:7.

Interview with Jane Kennedy,
Lead Mammal Keeper, San Diego Zoo Safari Park—August 10th, 2015

1. What is your most memorable moment with Nola?

Meeting Nola 26 years ago was amazing. While the Safari Park already had northern white rhinos and I had met them, I had never met a pair of females before. Both Nola, and her coalition partner Nadi, were so sweet. They were very gentle and they really wanted affection and love from the keepers. This is because, prior to coming to San Diego, these females were living in a traditional zoo where they had interaction with their keepers every day. Here at the Safari Park, we tend to let our animals live in a more naturalistic setting so that doesn't mean one-on-one interaction with rhinoceros'.

2. Is there something unique about Nola's personality that you would like to share?

Nola trusts humans, this is why: Nola has to have pedicures. Nola's nails grow unusually long and they grow a little bit up, that means she has to have them trimmed regularly. If Nola had not been brought into a captive situation she might have died as a young animal because of her nails. She has an odd gate because the nails affect the way that she walks, kind of flat footed. Unlike other rhinos, Nola isn't very fast. (Rhinos can run up to 35 miles an hour, you know!)

Our team of keepers very carefully approach Nola and two or three of us will rub her back and ears and she'll stay laying down while the other team members trim her nails. We always have a truck right next to us for safety because after all, Nola is a 4,000-pundgentle giant! Because she has always had her nail issue, she has always had this attention from her keepers, even when she lived in the Czech Republic. She learned over her lifetime to trust keepers and to know that we are there to take care of her and to help her. Her nail trims have become a part of her regular routine. Nola has learned to trust humans because all of the humans she's met in her entire life have always loved her and taken care of her.

3. What is Nola's favorite activity?

Nola's favorite thing to do is to be scratched and rubbed by her keepers! She loves it when we approach when she's lying down and we gently rub her. She loves to be scratched behind her ears and have her back rubbed with a scrub brush! She's an amazing animal.

4. How did Nola get her name?

Nola was given her name at her first zoo . . . Ironically, the meaning of the name Nola is famous champion, and Nola is the feminine form of Nolan. She is a champion for her species!

5. Why do you love rhinos, personally?

Rhinos are amazing prehistoric looking animals. When you first see them, they might scare you, but once you get to know them, you realize they're just gentle giants. Yes, they have power and strength, but they're also gentle. They're caring loving mothers, and the fathers here at the Safari Park play with their kids. Rhino bulls in the wild are also known to play with calves that they come across. Of course, the mother rhino is nearby to make sure things stay safe. It's easy to love and respect an animal that has that much power and that much grace and that much love to give.

You will always be loved little rhino, it's true Now and forever...I promise you!

Nola

Nola passed away peacefully on November 22, 2015
during the creation of our book.

She enjoyed a very long, happy life and was loved the world over.

Her passing was marked by everyone, from world leaders to her fans,
and most especially her Safari Park Family.

This gentle soul reminds us of what is best about courage,
spirit, trust and love.

Stephanie Lisa Tara
Pilar Lama
Tom Hamlyn

You will always be loved little rhino, it's true
Now and forever... I promise you!

Made in the USA
Middletown, DE
06 May 2016